This Is My Bank

Adam Bellamy

Enslow Publishing
101 W. 23rd Street
Suite 240
New York, NY 10011
USA

enslow.com

Published in 2017 by Enslow Publishing, LLC.
101 W. 23rd Street, Suite 240, New York, NY 10011

Library of Congress Cataloguing-in-Publication Data
Names: Bellamy, Adam, author.
Title: This is my bank / Adam Bellamy.
Description: New York, NY : Enslow Publishing, [2017] | Series: All about my world | Audience: Ages 5 up. | Audience: Pre-school, excluding K. | Includes bibliographical references and index.
Identifiers: LCCN 2016022714| ISBN 9780766081086 (library bound) | ISBN 9780766081062 (pbk.) | ISBN 9780766081079 (6-pack)
Subjects: LCSH: Banks and banking—Juvenile literature.
Classification: LCC HG1609 .B45 2017 | DDC 332.1—dc23
LC record available at https://lccn.loc.gov/2016022714

Printed in China

To Our Readers: We have done our best to make sure all websites in this book were active and appropriate when we went to press. However, the author and the publisher have no control over and assume no liability for the material available on those websites or on any websites they may link to. Any comments or suggestions can be sent by e-mail to customerservice@enslow.com.

Photo Credits: Cover, p. 1 Dzmitry Malyeuski/Shutterstock.com; peiyang/Shutterstock.com (globe icon on spine); pp. 3 (left), 8 Africa Studio/Shutterstock.com; pp. 3 (center), 18 Beth Ponticello/ Shutterstock.com; pp. 3 (right), 10, 12 © iStockphoto,com/YinYang; pp. 4–5 Frontpage/Shutterstock. com; p. 6 © iStockphoto.com/pawel gaul; p. 14 Blend Images-JGI/Jamie Grill/Brand X Pictures/Getty Images; p. 16 Peter Dazeley/Stone/Getty Images; p. 20 Dasha Petrenko/Shutterstock.com; p. 22 Erik Dreyer/The Image Bank/Getty Images.

Contents

Words to Know

cash   drive-through   teller

4

This is my bank.

People keep their money at the bank.

People also borrow money
from banks.

A teller will help me at the bank.

I can open an account to start saving money.

I can also exchange my coins for cash.

Now it's your turn

Rewrite an ending

Read the ending of your favorite adventure story. Are there other endings it could have had? Write one of them. Put it aside. Go back and read both versions later. Now which ending do you prefer, and why?

Have the last laugh

In *Two Weeks with the Queen*, Morris Gleitzman begins and ends with a wry joke about the Queen of England. These provide a comic frame for hero Colin's serious quest to find the world's best doctor to cure his brother. The final joke is the ultimate in upbeat endings. Read the book to find out why.

Create mixed emotions

The last lines of Anthony Horowitz's *Stormbreaker* have a dramatic, filmlike quality. Alex Rider watches the man who killed his uncle depart. His feelings are very mixed. Alex has solved the mystery, but he has not found the justice he craves. What other emotions does this ending evoke?

> *Behind the glass, [the assassin] raised his hand. A gesture of friendship? A salute? Alex raised his hand. The helicopter spun away. Alex stood where he was, watching it, until it had disappeared in the dying light.*
>
> Anthony Horowitz, *Stormbreaker*

TIPS AND TECHNIQUES

Good stories may seem to go in straight lines—beginning, middle, and end—but they also go around in circles. The hero returns to the place where he or she started but is now wiser.

MAKE YOUR WORDS WORK

Words are valuable things. Like water on a desert trek, you should use them sparingly and make every one count. In action-packed adventures, every word must work hard to carry the story forward.

Use vivid imagery

Metaphors and similes help readers to see a scene swiftly. In *King Solomon's Mines*, H. Rider Haggard uses a metaphor to describe some giraffes "which galloped or rather sailed off." In *Hoot*, Carl Hiaasen uses a simile, then a metaphor: "His legs felt like wet cement, and his lungs were on fire." In *The Kite Rider*, Geraldine McCaughrean uses the same idea as both a simile and a metaphor: "Jealousy, like a badly lit firework, fizzled and fumed in Haoyou's guts." In *Two Weeks with the Queen*, by Morris Gleitzman, a comic scene is used to relieve a tragic mood. Colin has gotten some bad news, and he defuses his anger and sorrow among the doctors' cars in the hospital parking lot:

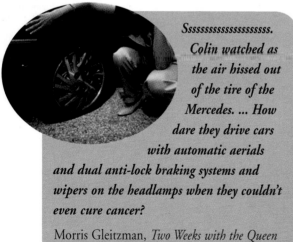

Sssssssssssssssssssss. Colin watched as the air hissed out of the tire of the Mercedes. ... How dare they drive cars with automatic aerials and dual anti-lock braking systems and wipers on the headlamps when they couldn't even cure cancer?

Morris Gleitzman, *Two Weeks with the Queen*

Now it's your turn

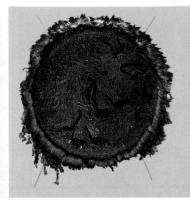

Work out with words

Give your vocabulary a workout. Brainstorm more lists. Come up with 30 adjectives and 30 nouns. Pair them randomly and see what you get: a blue-eyed boulder, a silken shield, or a frozen feather. Then reinvent well-known sayings. Don't say something is as white as snow. Say it is as white as a crocodile's grin or as an Arctic winter. Read the dictionary, too, and play word games.

Write with bite

When writing action scenes, choose words that sound most like the action you are describing—"smash" is more powerful than "hit," and "shriek" is more piercing than "cry."

Vary the length of your sentences, too. Try short ones for fast action and longer ones for lingering events.

Take a breath

Adventure stories are full of striving and struggling. Now and then, you need to give readers the chance to take a breather. Too much of anything can turn readers off. When they have had a break with some light relief, your return to your main mood (whether it is action or tragedy) will be much more effective.

TIPS AND TECHNIQUES

Increase suspense by building to an exciting moment. Give readers hints of the danger to come and then pounce. Or use foreshadowing—drop clues in advance about possible hazards.

USE DRAMATIC DIALOGUE

Dialogue lets readers "hear" your characters' own voices. It breaks up pages of solid print and gives readers' eyes a rest. When done well, dialogue can add color, pace, mood, and suspense to a story.

Let characters speak for themselves

The best way to learn about dialogue is to switch on your listening ear and eavesdrop. Listen to the way people phrase their sentences. Write down any good expressions. Did someone say "I'm ticked off" instead of "I'm angry"? Watch people's body language when they are whispering or arguing. Look, listen, and absorb.

Now it's your turn

Stand out

Tune in to a TV talk show. Spend 10 minutes writing down exactly what people say—including all the ums, ers, and repetitions. Listen for a range of voices: young, old, smart, foolish, angry, or cheery. Next compare it with some dialogue in a book. You will see at once that written dialogue does not include all the hesitations of natural speech, but it gives an impression of how people speak to one another.

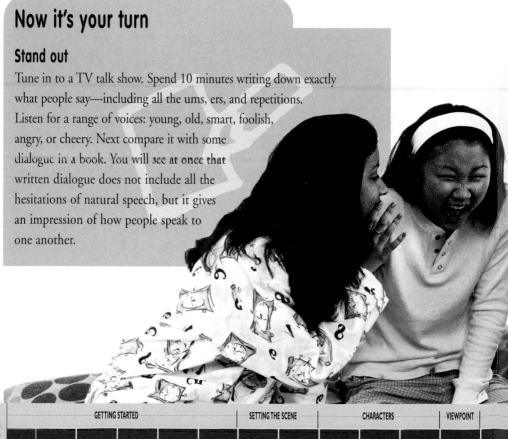

Banks keep the money in a locked room called a vault.

CLEARANCE: 11'-6"

Some banks have drive-throughs so you do not have to leave your car.

Banks have machines called ATMs. People use them to take out money.

Going to the bank can be fun!

Read More

Furgang, Kathy. *National Geographic Kids Everything Money*. Washington, DC: National Geographic Children's Books, 2013.

Kawa, Katie. *My First Trip to the Bank*. New York, NY: Gareth Stevens, 2012.

Larson, Jennifer S. *Where Do We Keep Money?: How Banks Work*. New York, NY: Lightning Bolt Books, 2010.

Websites

H.I.P. Pocket Change
www.usmint.gov/kids/
Official site of the US mint for kids.

TheMint.org
www.themint.org/kids/how-banks-work.html
Learn how banks work!

Index

Guided Reading Level: B
Guided Reading Leveling System is based on the guidelines recommended by Fountas and Pinnell.

Word Count: 85

APR 2017